# Summary

In 1994, Congress passed the Violence Against Women Act (VAWA, P.L. 103-322). The act was intended to change attitudes toward domestic violence, foster awareness of domestic violence, improve services and provisions for victims, and revise the manner in which the criminal justice system responds to domestic violence. This legislation created new programs within the Departments of Justice and Health and Human Services that aimed to both reduce domestic violence and improve response to and recovery from domestic violence incidents. VAWA primarily addresses certain types of violent crime through grant programs to state, tribal, and local governments; nonprofit organizations; and universities. VAWA programs target the crimes of intimate partner violence, dating violence, sexual assault, and stalking.

In 1995, the Office on Violence Against Women (OVW) was created administratively within the Department of Justice to administer federal grants authorized under VAWA. Since its creation, the OVW has awarded more than $3 billion in grants. While the OVW administers the majority of VAWA authorized grants, other federal agencies, including the Centers for Disease Control and Prevention and the Office of Justice Programs, also manage VAWA grants.

Since 1994, VAWA has been modified and reauthorized several times. In 2000, Congress reauthorized VAWA, enhanced federal domestic violence and stalking penalties, added protections for battered immigrants, and added new programs for elderly and disabled women. In 2005, Congress again reauthorized VAWA. The legislation enhanced penalties for repeat stalking offenders; added protections for battered and trafficked immigrants; and added programs for sexual assault victims and American Indian victims, and programs designed to improve the public health response to domestic violence.

Authorization for appropriations for the programs under VAWA expired in 2011. Several bills have been introduced in the 112th Congress that would reauthorize VAWA. On February 2, 2012, the Senate Judiciary Committee ordered reported the Violence Against Women Reauthorization Act of 2011 (S. 1925), and on April 26, the Senate amended and passed S. 1925. This bill was met with some opposition. For example, in the Senate Judiciary Committee Report (S.Rept. 112-153) and during the Executive Business Meeting of the Senate Judiciary Committee, concerns were raised regarding a proposed increase to the cap on the number of U-Visas available for immigrants; a proposed addition to the number of groups given special consideration as underserved populations; a proposed increase of jurisdictional power for American Indian tribes; and the accountability of OVW grantees.

On April 27, 2012, Representative Adams introduced the Violence Against Women Reauthorization Act of 2012 (H.R. 4970). It differs in substantive ways from S. 1925 including with respect to the VAWA-related immigration provisions and in the populations it would include under its definition of underserved population. H.R. 4970 was met with some opposition in the House. For example, concerns were raised during the markup of H.R. 4970 in the House Judiciary Committee with respect to new restrictions for immigration provisions under VAWA and the absence of special consideration for those who may be discriminated against based on gender identity or sexual orientation. Additionally, some Members sought increased jurisdictional powers for American Indian tribes, similar to provisions in S. 1925. On May 8, 2012, the House Judiciary Committee ordered reported H.R. 4970.

# Contents

Background and History of the Violence Against Women Act (VAWA) ........................................ 1

Violence Against Women Act of 1994 ........................................................................................... 2
    Investigations and Prosecutions ............................................................................................... 2
    Grant Programs ........................................................................................................................ 3
        Violence Prevention ........................................................................................................ 3
        Investigations and Prosecutions ..................................................................................... 3
        Victim Services ............................................................................................................... 3
    Other VAWA Requirements ..................................................................................................... 4
    Office on Violence Against Women ......................................................................................... 4
    Categories of Crime Addressed through VAWA ...................................................................... 4
    Reauthorizations of VAWA ...................................................................................................... 9
Reauthorization of VAWA and the 112th Congress ...................................................................... 10
    Selected Issues in the Reauthorization of VAWA in the 112th Congress ................................. 14

# Figures

Figure 1. Forcible Rapes Known to Police ...................................................................................... 8

# Tables

Table A-1. Descriptions of Current VAWA Authorized Programs under the Department of
    Justice (DOJ) and Department of Health and Human Services (HHS) ...................................... 17
Table A-2. FY2008-FY2012 Authorization and Appropriations for VAWA Programs .................. 23

# Appendixes

Appendix. Federal Programs Authorized by VAWA ...................................................................... 17

# Contacts

Author Contact Information ............................................................................................................. 35

# Background and History of the Violence Against Women Act (VAWA)

The Violence Against Women Act (VAWA), currently due for reauthorization, was originally passed by Congress as Title IV of the Violent Crime Control and Law Enforcement Act of 1994 (P.L. 103-322). This act addressed congressional concerns about violent crime, and in particular, violence against women, in several ways. Among other things, it enhanced investigations and prosecutions of sex offenses by allowing for enhanced sentencing of repeat federal sex offenders; mandating restitution to victims of specified federal sex offenses; and providing grants to state, local, and tribal law enforcement entities to investigate and prosecute violent crimes against women.

Congressional passage of VAWA was ultimately spurred on by decades of growing unease over the rising violent crime rate and a focus on women as crime victims. Beginning in the 1960s, the violent crime rate rose steadily,[1] igniting concern from both the public and the federal government. Supplementing the concern for the nation's rising violent crime rate was the concern for violence against women. In the 1970s, grassroots organizations began to stress the need for attitudinal change regarding violence against women. These organizations sought a change in attitude both among the public as well as the law enforcement community.[2]

In the 1980s, researchers began to address the violence against women issue as well. For instance, Straus and Gelles collected data on family violence and attributed declines in spousal assault to heightened awareness of the issue by both men and the criminal justice system.[3] The criminal justice system and the public were beginning to view family violence as a crime rather than a private family matter.[4]

In 1984, Congress enacted the Family Violence Prevention and Services Act (FVPSA, P.L. 98-457) to assist states in preventing incidents of family violence and to provide shelter and related assistance to victims of family violence and their dependents. While FVPSA authorized programs similar to those discussed in this report and has reauthorized programs that were originally created by VAWA, such as the National Domestic Violence Hotline, it is a separate piece of legislation and beyond the scope of this report.

In 1994, Congress passed a major crime bill, the Violent Crime Control and Law Enforcement Act of 1994.[5] Among other things, the bill created an unprecedented number of programs geared toward helping local law enforcement fight violent crime and servicing victims of violent crime.

---

[1] Kathleen Maguire and Ann Pastore, *Sourcebook of Criminal Justice Statistics 1994*, Bureau of Justice Statistics, Tables 3.108, 3.131, http://www.albany.edu/sourcebook/pdf/sb1994/sb1994-section3.pdf; and U.S. Department of Justice, Federal Bureau of Investigation, *Crime in the United States*, http://www fbi.gov/about-us/cjis/ucr/ucr. Violent crimes include murders, non-negligent manslaughters, and aggravated assaults.

[2] Kimberley D. Bailey, "Lost in Translation: Domestic Violence, "the Personal is Political," and the Criminal Justice System.," *Journal of Criminal Law & Criminology*, vol. 100, no. 4 (Fall 2010), pp. 1255-1300.

[3] Murray Straus and Richard Gelles, "Societal Change and Change in Family Violence from 1975 to 1985," *Journal of Marriage and Family*, vol. 48, Iss. 3, August 1986.

[4] Ibid.

[5] National Institute of Justice, *Violent Crime Control and Law Enforcement Act of 1994*, http://www nij.gov/pubs-sum/000067 htm.

---

In their introduction of the Violence Against Women Act, then-Senator Joseph Biden and Senator Barbara Boxer highlighted the weak legal response to violence against women by police and prosecutors.[6] The shortfalls of legal response and the need for a change in attitudes toward violence against women were primary reasons cited for the passage of VAWA.[7]

Since it was enacted in 1994, Congress has twice reauthorized VAWA. The most recent authorization of appropriations for VAWA programs expired in FY2011. These programs, however, have continued to receive funding. On April 26, 2012 the Senate amended and passed the Violence Against Women Reauthorization Act of 2011 (S. 1925). On May 8, 2012, the House Judiciary Committee favorably reported the Violence Against Women Reauthorization Act of 2012 (H.R. 4970).

This report provides a brief legislative history of VAWA and an overview of the crimes addressed through VAWA. It then discusses legislation that would reauthorize VAWA and selected issues. The **Appendix** of this report outlines funding information for VAWA authorized programs from FY2008 through FY2012.

# Violence Against Women Act of 1994

As mentioned, VAWA was originally passed by Congress as part of the broader Violent Crime Control and Law Enforcement Act of 1994. The Violence Against Women Act of 1994 (1) enhanced investigations and prosecutions of sex offenses and (2) provided for a number of grant programs to address the issue of violence against women from a variety of angles including law enforcement, public and private entities and service providers, and victims of crime. The sections below highlight examples of these VAWA provisions.

## Investigations and Prosecutions

As passed in 1994, VAWA impacted federal investigations and prosecutions of cases involving violence against women in a number of ways. For instance, it established new offenses and penalties for the violation of a protection order as well as stalking in which an abuser crossed a state line to injure or harass another, or forced a victim to cross a state line under duress and then physically harmed the victim in the course of a violent crime. It also added new provisions to require states and territories to enforce protection orders issued by other states, tribes and territories. VAWA also allowed for enhanced sentencing of repeat federal sex offenders. It also authorized funding for the Attorney General to develop training programs to assist probation and parole officers to work with released sex offenders.

In addition, VAWA established a new requirement for pretrial detention in federal sex offense or child pornography felony cases. It also modified the Federal Rules of Evidence to include new procedures specifying that, with few exceptions, a victim's past sexual behavior was not

---

[6] Senators Biden and Boxer, "Violence Against Women," Remarks in the Senate, *Congressional Record*, June 21, 1994.

[7] Joseph Biden, "Violence Against Women: The Congressional Response," *American Psychologist*, vol. 48, no. 10 (October 1993), pp. 1059-1061; Barbara Vobejda, "Battered Women's Cry Relayed Up From Grass Roots," *The Washington Post*, July 6, 1994, p. A1.

admissible in federal and civil cases of sexual misconduct.[8] In addition, VAWA asked the Attorney General to study measures in place to ensure confidentiality between sexual assault or domestic violence victims and their counselors.

VAWA mandated restitution to victims of specified federal sex offenses, specifically sexual abuse as well as sexual exploitation and other abuse of children. It also established new provisions, including a civil remedy that allows victims of sexual assault to seek civil penalties from their alleged assailants,[9] and a provision that allows rape victims to demand that their alleged assailants be tested for the HIV virus.

# Grant Programs

VAWA created a number of grant programs and authorized funding for the programs for a range of activities including violence prevention, investigations and prosecutions, and victim services.

## Violence Prevention

For instance, under VAWA, grants were authorized for capital improvements to prevent crime in public transportation systems as well as in public and national parks. It also expanded the Family Violence Prevention and Services Act (FVPSA)[10] to include grants for youth education on domestic violence and intimate partner violence as well as to include grants for community intervention and prevention programs.

## Investigations and Prosecutions

As mentioned, VAWA provided for federal grants to state, local, and tribal law enforcement entities to investigate and prosecute violent crimes against women. It established an additional grant to bolster investigations and prosecutions in rural areas. It also established a grant program to encourage state, local, and tribal arrest policies in domestic violence cases.

VAWA authorized grants for education and training for judges and court personnel in state and federal courts on the laws of rape, sexual assault, domestic violence, and other crimes of violence motivated by the victim's gender. It also authorized grants to assist state and local governments to enter data on stalking and domestic violence into national databases.

## Victim Services

VAWA authorized the expansion of the Public Health Service Act[11] to include purpose areas for rape prevention education. Additionally, it expanded the purpose areas of the Runaway and Homeless Youth Act[12] to allow for grant funding to assist youth at risk of (or who have been

---

[8] Fed. R. Evid. 412.

[9] In 2000, the U.S. Supreme Court struck down a provision of VAWA that allowed for a civil remedy for victims of gender-based violence. For more information, see *U.S. v. Morrison*, 529 U.S. 598 (2000).

[10] 42 U.S.C. §10401 et seq.

[11] 42 U.S.C. §280b et seq.

[12] 42 U.S.C. §5711 et seq.

subjected to) sexual abuse. VAWA reauthorized the Court-Appointed Special Advocate Program and the Child Abuse Training Programs for Judicial Personnel and Practitioners. It also authorized funding for Grants for Televised Testimony by Victims of Child Abuse.

VAWA established the National Domestic Violence Hotline and authorized funding for its operation.[13] It also authorized funding for battered women's shelters. VAWA also included special protections for battered immigrant women and children.[14]

## Other VAWA Requirements

Beyond the criminal justice improvements and grant programs, VAWA included provisions for several other activities including

- requiring that the U.S. Postal Service take measures to ensure confidentiality of domestic violence shelters and abused persons' addresses;

- mandating federal research by the Attorney General, National Academy of Sciences, and Secretary of Health and Human Services to increase the government's understanding of violence against women; and

- requesting special studies on campus sexual assault and battered women's syndrome.

## Office on Violence Against Women

In 1995, the Office on Violence Against Women (OVW) was administratively created within DOJ to administer the grants authorized under VAWA.[15] Since its creation, the OVW has awarded more than $4.7 billion in grants and cooperative agreements to state, tribal, and local governments, nonprofit organizations, and universities.[16] While the OVW administers the majority of VAWA authorized grants, other federal agencies, including the Centers for Disease Control and Prevention (CDC) and the Office of Justice Programs (OJP), also manage VAWA funds. See **Table A-1** for an outline of current VAWA authorized grant programs.

## Categories of Crime Addressed through VAWA

VAWA grant programs address the needs of victims of domestic violence, sexual assault, dating violence, and stalking. VAWA treats these as distinct crimes which involve a wide range of victim demographics. For domestic violence, sexual assault, and stalking, the risk of victimization is

---

[13] The National Domestic Violence Hotline is now authorized by FVPSA (P.L. 111-320) and codified at 42 U.S.C. §10413.

[14] For more information, see CRS Report R42477, *Immigration Provisions of the Violence Against Women Act (VAWA)*, by William A. Kandel.

[15] In 2002, OVW was codified through Title IV of the 21st Century Department of Justice Appropriations Authorization Act (P.L. 107-273).

[16] U.S. Department of Justice, Office on Violence Against Women, *About the Office*, http://www.ovw.usdoj.gov/overview.htm.

highest for women.[17] For dating violence, the risk of victimization is the same for both men and women.[18]

Victimization data on these crimes are available from two national surveys, the National Crime Victimization Survey (NCVS) and the Youth Risk Behavior Surveillance System[19] and the Federal Bureau of Investigation's (FBI's) Uniform Crime Reporting (UCR) Program.[20] UCR data vary from survey data because the UCR describes crimes that were reported to law enforcement while survey data describe self-reported crimes that were not necessarily reported to law enforcement. Due to differences in methodology, survey data are not comparable to UCR data.[21]

## Domestic Violence

As discussed, public concern over violence against women prompted the original passage of VAWA. As such, VAWA legislation and programs have historically emphasized women as victims. More recently, however, there has been a focus on ensuring the needs of all victims are met through provisions of VAWA programs.[22]

Domestic violence is a complex crime and is often labeled as family violence or intimate partner violence. Under VAWA, domestic violence is generally interpreted as intimate partner violence. Intimate partner violence includes felony or misdemeanor crimes committed by spouses or ex-spouses, boyfriends or girlfriends, and ex-boyfriends or ex-girlfriends. Crimes may include sexual assault, simple or aggravated assault, and homicide. As defined in statute for the purposes of VAWA grant programs, domestic violence includes

> felony or misdemeanor crimes of violence committed by a current or former spouse of the victim, by a person with whom the victim shares a child in common, by a person who is cohabiting with or has cohabited with the victim as a spouse, by a person similarly situated to a spouse of the victim under the domestic or family violence laws of the jurisdiction receiving grant monies, or by any other person against an adult or youth victim

---

[17] Shannan Catalano, Erica Smith, Howard Snyder, and Michael Rand, U.S. Department of Justice, Bureau of Justice Statistics, *Female Victims of Violence*, September 2009, http://bjs.ojp.usdoj.gov/content/pub/pdf/fvv.pdf (hereinafter *Female Victims of Violence*, 2009); and Katrina Baum, Shannan Catalano, and Michael Rand, U.S. Department of Justice, Bureau of Justice Statistics, *Stalking Victimization in the United States*, January 2009, http://bjs.ojp.usdoj.gov/content/pub/pdf/svus.pdf (hereinafter *Stalking Victimization in the United States*, 2009).

[18] The Centers for Disease Control and Prevention, *Selected Health Risk Behaviors and Health Outcomes by Sex, National YRBS: 2009*, http://www.cdc.gov/healthyyouth/yrbs/pdf/us_disparitysex_yrbs.pdf.

[19] U.S. Department of Health and Human Services, The Centers for Disease Control, *Youth Risk Behavior Surveillance System (YRBSS)*, http://www.cdc.gov/healthyyouth/yrbs/; and U.S. Department of Justice, Office of Justice Programs, Bureau of Justice Statistics, *National Crime Victimization Survey*, http://bjs.ojp.usdoj.gov/index.cfm?ty=dcdetail&iid=245.

[20] U.S. Department of Justice, Federal Bureau of Investigation, *Uniform Crime Reporting Program*, http://www.fbi.gov/about-us/cjis/ucr/ucr.

[21] For additional information regarding the differences in crime data collection and limitations of the data, see CRS Report RL34309, *How Crime in the United States Is Measured*, by Nathan James and Logan Rishard Council. For a comparison of methodologies used by the UCR and National Crime Victimization Survey, see *The Nation's Two Crime Measures*, http://bjs.ojp.usdoj.gov/content/pub/pdf/ntcm.pdf.

[22] U.S. Congress, House Committee on the Judiciary, Subcommittee on Crime, Terrorism, and Homeland Security, *Hearing on: the U.S. Department of Justice, Office on Violence Against Women*, Testimony by Susan Carbon, 112th Cong., 2nd sess., February 16, 2012.

---

who is protected from that person's acts under the domestic or family violence laws of the jurisdiction.[23]

Data from the NCVS indicate that the rate of intimate partner violence is approximately four times higher for females than males.[24] There were 407,700 females that reported victimization by an intimate partner (3.1 per 1,000 persons aged 12 and older) in 2010, compared to 101,530 males (0.8 per 1,000 persons aged 12 and older) who reported victimization by an intimate partner. According to NCVS data, intimate partner victimization rates also vary by age and race. Females aged 18 or older generally experience higher rates of intimate partner violence than females aged 12 to 17. Rates of intimate partner violence have also been historically higher for black females than white females.[25]

In 2010, a survey conducted by the Centers for Disease Control and Prevention included questions about lifetime victimization. The CDC estimates that 24.3% of women (one in four women) and 13.8% of men (one in seven men) have experienced severe physical violence[26] by an intimate partner in their lifetime.[27]

## Intimate Partner Homicide

Since peaking in the early 1990s, the violent and property crime rates have declined. Overall homicide rates and intimate partner homicide rates have also declined. Researchers have studied the range of social factors that may influence homicide rates and have suggested possible reasons for the decline in intimate partner homicide rates. For instance, most intimate partner homicides involve married couples; as such, some researchers have suggested the decline in marriage rates among young adults as a contributing factor in the decline in intimate partner homicide rates.[28] Additionally, divorce and separation rates have increased. Fewer marriages may result in less exposure to abusive partners and fewer marriages may suggest that those who do marry are more selective in choosing a partner.[29]

Homicide is committed largely by males, mostly victimizing males. From 1980 through 2008, males made up 90% of all offenders and 77% of all homicide victims; however, females were more likely than males to be victims of intimate partner homicide.[30] From 1980 through 2008,

---

[23] 42 U.S.C. §13925.

[24] U.S. Department of Justice, Bureau of Justice Statistics, *Criminal Victimization, 2010*, p.10, http://bjs.ojp.usdoj.gov/content/pub/pdf/cv10.pdf.

[25] Ibid, p. 2.

[26] The CDC provided the following examples of severe physical violence: "hit with a fist or something hard, beaten, [or] slammed against something."

[27] The Centers for Disease Control and Prevention, *National Intimate Partner Sexual Violence Survey, 2010 Summary Report*, November 2011, p. 2, http://www.cdc.gov/ViolencePrevention/pdf/NISVS_Executive_Summary-a.pdf (hereinafter *National Intimate Partner Sexual Violence Survey, 2010*).

[28] Laura Dugan, Daniel Nagin, and Richard Rosenfeld, Do Domestic Violence Services Save Lives?, *National Institute of Justice Journal*, Issue 250 (November 2003), p. 22, https://www.ncjrs.gov/pdffiles1/jr000250f.pdf.

[29] Ibid.

[30] Margaret Zahn, Intimate Partner Homicide: An Overview, *National Institute of Justice Journal*, Issue 250 (November 2003), p. 2; and Bureau of Justice Statistics, *Homicide Trends in the United States, 1980-2008*, November 2011, pp. 3, 18, http://bjs.ojp.usdoj.gov/content/pub/pdf/htus8008.pdf (hereinafter *Homicide Trends in the United States*).

female homicide victims were six times more likely than male victims to have been a victim of intimate partner homicide, and 63% of all intimate partner homicide victims were female.[31]

## Sexual Assault

While intimate partner violence can, and often does, include sexual assault,[32] it is viewed as a separate category of crime under VAWA. Sexual assault may include the crimes of forcible rape, attempted forcible rape, assault with intent to rape, statutory rape, and other sexual offenses. Sexual assault is not defined in the U.S. Code, but other associated crimes, such as sexual abuse and aggravated sexual abuse, are defined in the U.S. Code.[33] Under VAWA, sexual assault includes any conduct that may be described as sexual abuse or aggravated sexual abuse.

According to statistics from the NCVS, there were 184,390 sexual assaults in 2010.[34] These data are not comprehensive because some victimizations are not reported to law enforcement. Moreover, these data are not comparable to UCR data because the NCVS includes male victims in its definition of sexual assault, and UCR statistics from 2010 do not include male victims.

According to the FBI's UCR Program, 84,767 forcible rapes were reported to law enforcement in 2010. Since 1991, when 106,593 forcible rapes were reported to law enforcement, this figure has fluctuated but has declined overall, as illustrated in **Figure 1**.

---

[31] *Homicide Trends in the United States*, p. 10.

[32] *Female Victims of Violence*, 2009. p. 2.

[33] 42 U.S.C. §13925; 18 U.S.C. §2241 et seq.

[34] U.S. Department of Justice, Bureau of Justice Statistics, *Criminal Victimization, 2010*, September 2011, p. 9, http://bjs.ojp.usdoj.gov/content/pub/pdf/cv10.pdf.

## Figure 1. Forcible Rapes Known to Police

### (1991–2010)

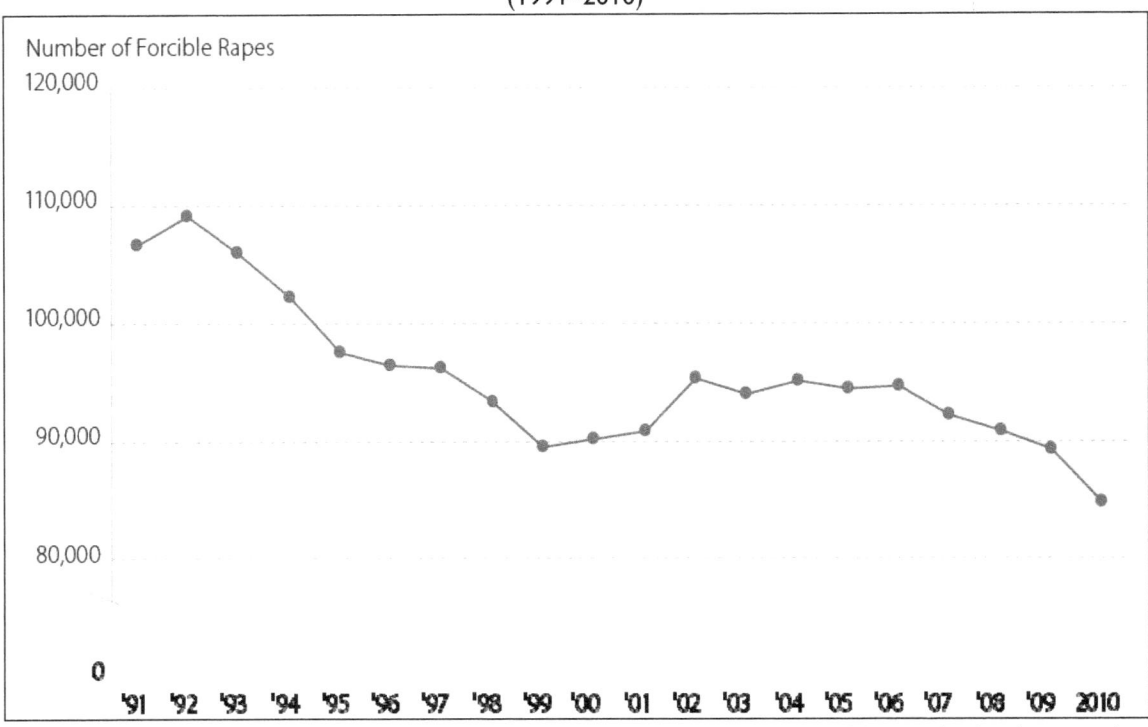

**Source:** CRS presentation of UCR data. These data are available at http://www.fbi.gov/about-us/cjis/ucr/crime-in-the-u.s/2010/crime-in-the-u.s.-2010/tables/10tbl01.xls.

**Note:** These data include only female victims; from 1991-2010 the FBI definition of rape did not include male victims.

Through 2010, the FBI defined forcible rape as, "the carnal knowledge of a female forcibly and against her will."[35] Forcible rape statistics include attempted forcible rape and assault with intent to rape, but exclude statutory rape without force and other sex offenses.[36] In January 2012, the FBI revised its definition of forcible rape to include male victims.[37] Future UCR reports will include rape statistics for male victims.

## Dating Violence

Under VAWA, dating violence refers to "violence committed by a person who is or has been in a social relationship of a romantic or intimate nature with the victim."[38] The relationship between the offender and victim is determined based on the following factors: (1) the length of the relationship; (2) the type of relationship; and (3) the frequency of interaction between the persons involved in the relationship.[39]

---

[35] U.S. Department of Justice, Federal Bureau of Investigation, *Crime in the United States, 2010*, September 2011, p.1, http://www.fbi.gov/about-us/cjis/ucr/crime-in-the-u.s/2010/crime-in-the-u.s.-2010/violent-crime/rapemain.pdf.

[36] Ibid.

[37] U.S. Department of Justice, Office of Public Affairs, *Attorney General Eric Holder Announces Revisions to the Uniform Crime Report's Definition of Rape*, http://www.justice.gov/opa/pr/2012/January/12-ag-018 html.

[38] 42 U.S.C. §13925.

[39] Ibid.

---

Reports on dating violence usually refer to teenagers as the relevant age demographic. According to the *2009 Youth Risk Behavior Survey*, approximately 10% of high school students had been "hit, slapped, or physically hurt on purpose by their boyfriend or girlfriend" in the past year.[40] Unlike other crimes addressed by VAWA, females were just as likely as males to report this outcome.[41]

## Stalking

Stalking is defined as "a course of conduct directed at a specific person that would cause a reasonable person to feel fear."[42] All 50 states, the District of Columbia, and U.S. Territories have enacted anti-stalking laws, and these laws vary in their definition.[43] Federal law makes it unlawful to (1) travel across state lines or use the mail or computer; (2) with the intent to injure or harass another; and (3) as a result, places that person in reasonable fear of death or serious bodily injury or causes substantial emotional distress to that person or a member of that person's family.[44]

According to the NCVS, 3.4 million individuals aged 18 and older were victims of stalking in 2006.[45] Females were at greater risk than males for stalking victimization, and individuals aged 18-24 were at greater risk than those individuals aged 25 or older.[46] According to the CDC, 10.7% of women and 2.1% of men have been stalked by an intimate partner in their lifetime.[47]

# Reauthorizations of VAWA

Since it was enacted in 1994, Congress has twice reauthorized VAWA. Of note, both reauthorizations had broad bipartisan support.[48]

- In 2000, Congress reauthorized VAWA through the Victims of Trafficking and Violence Protection Act (P.L. 106-386). Modifications included additional protections for battered immigrants,[49] a new program for victims in need of transitional housing, a requirement for grant recipients to submit reports on the effectiveness of programs, new programs designed to protect elderly and disabled women, mandatory funds to be used exclusively for rape prevention and education programs, and inclusion of victims of dating violence.[50] VAWA 2000

---

[40] The Centers for Disease Control and Prevention, *Selected Health Risk Behaviors and Health Outcomes by Sex National YRBS: 2009*, http://www.cdc.gov/healthyyouth/yrbs/pdf/us_disparitysex_yrbs.pdf.

[41] Ibid.

[42] *Stalking Victimization in the United States*, 2009, p. 1.

[43] Ibid.

[44] 18 U.S.C. §2261(A).

[45] In 2006, the NCVS included a supplemental survey that identified victims of stalking.

[46] *Stalking Victimization in the United States*, 2009, pp. 2-3.

[47] *National Intimate Partner Sexual Violence Survey*, 2010, p. 2.

[48] In 2000, the House passed the Victims of Trafficking and Violence Protection Act of 2000 (P.L. 106-386) with a 371-1 vote and the Senate unanimously passed the bill. In 2005, the House passed the Violence Against Women and Department of Justice Reauthorization Act of 2005 (P.L. 109-162) with a 415-4 vote, and the Senate again unanimously passed the bill.

[49] For more information, see CRS Report R42477, *Immigration Provisions of the Violence Against Women Act (VAWA)*, by William A. Kandel.

[50] The term "dating violence" was not used in the original VAWA and was added in VAWA 2000.

amended interstate stalking and domestic violence law to include (1) a person who travels in interstate or foreign commerce with the intent to kill, injure, harass, or intimidate a spouse or intimate partner, and who in the course of such travel commits or attempts to commit a crime of violence against the spouse or intimate partner; (2) a person who causes a spouse or intimate partner to travel in interstate or foreign commerce by force or coercion and in the course of such travel commits or attempts to commit a crime of violence against the spouse or intimate partner; (3) a person who travels in interstate or foreign commerce with the intent of violating a protection order or causes a person to travel in interstate or foreign commerce by force or coercion and violates a protection order; and (4) a person who uses the mail or any facility of interstate or foreign commerce to engage in a course of conduct that would place a person in reasonable fear of harm to themselves or their immediate family or intimate partner.[51] Also, the act added the intimate partners of victims as people covered under the interstate stalking statute.

- In 2005, Congress reauthorized VAWA through the Violence Against Women and Department of Justice Reauthorization Act (P.L. 109-162).[52] The legislation added protections for battered and trafficked immigrants,[53] enhanced penalties for repeat stalking offenders, added programs for American Indian victims, sexual assault victims and programs designed to improve the public health response to domestic violence. The act emphasized collaboration among law enforcement; health and housing professionals; and women, men, and youth alliances, and encourages community initiatives to address these issues.

# Reauthorization of VAWA and the 112th Congress

Several bills have been introduced in the 112th Congress that would reauthorize appropriations for programs under VAWA. On November 30, 2011, Senator Leahy introduced the Violence Against Women Reauthorization Act of 2011 (S. 1925).[54] On February 2, 2012, the Senate Judiciary Committee ordered favorably reported S. 1925, and on March 12, 2012, the committee filed a written report (S.Rept. 112-153) to accompany the bill. On April 26, the Senate amended and passed S. 1925. On April 27, 2012, Representative Adams introduced the Violence Against Women Reauthorization Act of 2012 (H.R. 4970). On May 8, 2012, H.R. 4970 was favorably reported by the House Judiciary Committee on May 8, 2012.[55]

---

[51] 18 U.S.C. §2261 and §2262.

[52] Provisions in VAWA 2005 were modified in A Bill to Make Technical Corrections to the Violence Against Women and Department of Justice Reauthorization Act of 2005 (P.L. 109-271).

[53] For more information, see CRS Report R42477, *Immigration Provisions of the Violence Against Women Act (VAWA)*, by William A. Kandel.

[54] One alternative reauthorization bill was introduced in the Senate. On April 23, 2012, Senator Hutchison introduced the Violence Against Women Reauthorization Act of 2012 (S. 2338). The bill was ordered placed on Senate Legislative Calendar under general orders.

[55] Two alternative reauthorization bills have been introduced in the House. On March 27, 2012, Representative Moore introduced the Violence Against Women Reauthorization Act of 2012 (H.R. 4271). The bill was referred to the House Committees on the Judiciary, Energy and Commerce, Education and the Workforce, Financial Services, and Natural Resources. On April 27, 2012, Representative Biggert introduced the Violence Against Women Reauthorization Act of 2012 (H.R. 4982). The bill was referred to the House Committees on the Judiciary, Energy and Commerce, Education (continued...)

---

## Selected Similarities Between S. 1925 and H.R. 4970

Both S. 1925 and H.R. 4970 would, among other things,

- reauthorize most VAWA grant programs and authorize appropriations at a lower level, in general, then their previous authorizations;

- consolidate VAWA grant programs that support families in the justice system and strengthen the healthcare system's response to domestic violence, dating violence, and stalking;

- repeal four VAWA grant programs (*Interdisciplinary Training and Education on Domestic Violence and Other Types of Violence and Abuse [42 U.S.C. 294H]; Research on effective interventions in the health care setting [42 U.S.C. 13973]; Development of curricula and pilot programs for home visitation projects [42 U.S.C. 14043d-3]; Engaging men and youth in preventing domestic violence, dating violence, sexual assault, and stalking [42 U.S.C. 14043d-4]; and Public awareness campaign [42 U.S.C. 14045c)*;

- reduce the overall annual authorization level for VAWA grant programs;[56]

- establish new audit requirements for VAWA grantees;

- enhance protection of personally identifiable information of victims;[57]

- include victims of dating violence in the Transitional Housing Assistance Grant Program and ensure that victims are not subject to prohibited activities, including background checks or clinical evaluations, to determine eligibility for services;

- promote additional housing rights for victims of domestic violence, dating violence, sexual assault, and stalking, including a provision that states that an applicant may not be denied public housing on the basis that the person has been a victim of domestic violence, dating violence, sexual assault, and stalking;

- redefine "linguistically and culturally specific services" by removing "linguistically" from the term, and changing the definition to address the needs of culturally specific communities rather than underserved communities;

- add the terms "population specific services" and "population specific organizations" so as to include these services and organizations as eligible entities under VAWA;[58]

---

(...continued)

and the Workforce, Financial Services, and Natural Resources.

[56] The authorization levels for each existing VAWA grant program will either decrease or remain the same.

[57] While both S. 1925 and H.R. 4970 would allow sharing of law enforcement-generated and prosecution-generated information necessary for law enforcement or prosecution, H.R. 4970 differs from S. 1925 in that it also allows sharing of law enforcement-generated and prosecution-generated information necessary for intelligence or national security.

[58] S. 1925 and H.R. 4970 define a population specific organization as a "nonprofit, nongovernmental organization that primarily serves members of a specific underserved population and has demonstrated experience and expertise providing targeted services to members of that specific underserved population."

S. 1925 and H.R. 4970 define population specific services as "victim-centered services that address the safety, health, economic, legal, housing, workplace, immigration, confidentiality, or other needs of victims of domestic violence, dating violence, sexual assault, or stalking, and that are designed primarily for and are targeted to a specific (continued...)

---

- amend federal law to include a mandatory minimum sentence for aggravated sexual abuse by force or threat (*S. 1925 would create a five-year mandatory minimum penalty wherein H.R. 4970 would create a 10-year mandatory minimum penalty*);[59]

- establish a nondiscrimination provision for all VAWA grant programs to ensure that victims are not denied services on the basis of race, color, religion, national origin, sex, or disability (*S. 1925 would also include gender identity and sexual orientation*);

- expand the purpose areas of several VAWA grants to address the needs of sexual assault survivors to include strengthening law enforcement and forensic response and urging jurisdictions to evaluate and reduce rape kit backlogs;

- establish a new requirement that at least 20% of funds within the STOP (Services, Training, Officers, Prosecutors) Program and 25% of funds within the Grants to Encourage Arrest Policies and Enforce Protection Orders Program be directed to programs that meaningfully address sexual assault;

- define "individual in later life" to mean a person who is is 50 years of age or older (S. 1925) and 60 years of age or older (H.R. 4970).

- enhance criminal penalties for assaulting a spouse, intimate partner, or dating partner;[60]

- enhance criminal penalties for criminal and civil rights violations involving sexual abuse;

- expand the purpose areas of grants to tribal governments and coalitions to include sex trafficking; and

- amend rules for sexual acts in federal custodial facilities by adding "the commission of a sexual act" as grounds for civil action by a federal prisoner and mandating that detention facilities operated by the Department of Homeland Security and custodial facilities operated by the Department of Health and Human Services adopt national standards set forth through the Prison Rape Elimination Act of 2003 (P.L. 108-79).

## Selected Differences Between S. 1925 and H.R. 4970

In contrast to H.R. 4970, **S. 1925 would**

- redefine "underserved populations" to include those who may be discriminated against based on religion, sexual orientation or gender identity;[61]

---

(...continued)

underserved population."

[59] 18 U.S.C. §2241(a).

[60] 42 U.S.C. §113.

[61] 42 U.S.C. §13925 defines underserved populations as "populations underserved because of geographic location, underserved racial and ethnic populations, populations underserved because of special needs (such as language barriers, disabilities, alienage status, or age), and any other population determined to be underserved by the Attorney General or by the Secretary of Health and Human Services, as appropriate."

- require the OVW to establish a biennial conferral process with grantees and key stakeholders;[62]

- expand provisions for battered immigrants including an increase in the cap on the number of U-Visas available for immigrants;[63]

- establish new mandatory grant guidelines for campuses and universities in their incident response procedures and development of programs to prevent domestic violence, sexual assault, stalking, and dating violence;

- expand the definition of cyberstalking to include use of "any electronic communication device or electronic communication system of interstate commerce;"

- amend the Immigration and Nationality Act to include a third drunk driving offense as an aggravated felony for the purposes of removing a noncitizen from the United States;[64] and

- expand the purpose areas of grants for American Indian tribal governments and coalitions to raise awareness of and response to domestic violence to include identifying and providing technical assistance to enhance access to services for Indian women victims of domestic and sexual violence, including sex trafficking.

S. 1925 would also address jurisdictional issues on tribal lands. It would grant American Indian tribes criminal jurisdiction over domestic violence, dating violence, and violations of protective orders that occur on tribal lands when certain criteria are met.[65] The bill would also grant tribes civil jurisdiction to issue and enforce protection orders. Moreover, the bill would add a new grant program to support tribal efforts to combat domestic violence.

In contrast to S. 1925, **H.R. 4970 would**

- amend the DNA Backlog Elimination Act of 2000 to establish that not less than 75% of VAWA funds be directed to the collection of DNA samples;[66]

- place new restrictions on immigration provisions under VAWA;[67]

- establish a new requirement for grant recipients that educational programming, training, or public awareness communications regarding domestic violence, dating violence, sexual assault, or stalking must be evidence-based;

---

[62] The areas of conferral will include (1) the administration of grants, (2) unmet needs. (3) promising practices in the field, and (4) emerging trends. After the conferral with grantees, OVW must publish a comprehensive report that summarizes the issues presented and what, if any, policies it intends to implement to address those issues.

[63] For additional information, see CRS Report R42477, *Immigration Provisions of the Violence Against Women Act (VAWA)*, by William A. Kandel.

[64] 8 U.S.C. §1101(a)(43)(F).

[65] Tribes do not currently have criminal jurisdiction over non-Indians (*Oliphant v. Suquamish Indian Tribe*, 435 U.S. (191, 210 1978). S. 1925 would expand tribal courts' criminal jurisdiction over non-Indians for crimes of domestic violence. For additional information, see CRS Report R42488, *Tribal Criminal Jurisdiction over Non-Indians in the Violence Against Women Act (VAWA) Reauthorization and the SAVE Native Women Act*, by Jane M. Smith and Richard M. Thompson II.

[66] The DNA Backlog Elimination Act of 2000 is codified in 42 U.S.C. § 14135 et seq.

[67] For additional information related to immigration provisions under VAWA, see CRS Report R42477, *Immigration Provisions of the Violence Against Women Act (VAWA)*, by William A. Kandel.

---

- prohibit grant recipients from lobbying government personnel regarding the award of grant funding;

- define "child" to mean a person who is under 11 years of age;

- redefine "underserved populations" to include those who may be discriminated against based on religion, but in contrast to S. 1925, would *not* include those who may be discriminated against *based on sexual orientation or gender identity*;[68]

- amend current law to include a five-year mandatory minimum sentence for aggravated sexual abuse by other means;[69]

- amend the Immigration and Nationality Act to allow the Attorney General to consider other reliable evidence in determining offense of domestic violence, stalking, and child abuse, including police reports and sentencing reports, for the purposes of removing a noncitizen from the United States; and

- authorize the Director of the Office of Community Oriented Policing Services to establish and operate a National Center for Campus Public Safety to address campus violence prevention and response.

## Selected Issues in the Reauthorization of VAWA in the 112th Congress

The reauthorization of VAWA (S. 1925) was met with some opposition in the Senate. Several concerns were raised in the Senate Judiciary Committee Report (S.Rept. 112-153) and during the Executive Business Meeting of the Senate Judiciary Committee, including

- the proposed increase to the cap on the number of U-Visas available for immigrants;

- the proposed addition to the number of groups given special consideration as underserved populations;

- the proposed increase of jurisdictional power for American Indian tribes; and

- the accountability of OVW grantees.

S. 1925 proposes to increase the cap on the number of U-Visas available for battered immigrants.[70] U-Visas grant nonimmigrant status to immigrants who are victims of domestic violence and are willing to assist authorities in the investigation and prosecution of their attackers.[71] Some Members have voiced concern over the expansion of immigration laws.[72]

---

[68] 42 U.S.C. §13925 defines underserved populations as "populations underserved because of geographic location, underserved racial and ethnic populations, populations underserved because of special needs (such as language barriers, disabilities, alienage status, or age), and any other population determined to be underserved by the Attorney General or by the Secretary of Health and Human Services, as appropriate."

[69] 18 U.S.C. §2241(b).

[70] The legislation proposes to recapture unused visas that were available and not issued to immigrants from 2006 – 2011. For additional information regarding U-Visas and VAWA provisions related to immigrant status, see For additional information, see CRS Report R42477, *Immigration Provisions of the Violence Against Women Act (VAWA)*, by William A. Kandel.

[71] 8 U.S.C. §1101(a)(15).

An additional issue raised in opposition to S. 1925 is the proposal to add persons who may be discriminated against based on sexual orientation or gender identity as an "underserved population" under VAWA. Critics contend that more data are needed to verify groups as underserved. They also contend that VAWA will have too many groups for special consideration and will lose its focus on overall victim assistance.[73]

S. 1925 proposes to increase jurisdictional power for American Indian tribes, and this was an issue cited in opposition to the bill.[74] Tribes do not currently have criminal jurisdiction over non-American Indians. The proposed legislation seeks to grant criminal jurisdiction over non-American Indians in cases of domestic violence. Concerns were raised over this change because (1) it would represent an unprecedented expansion of tribal jurisdiction; and (2) defendants may not receive the full panoply of constitutional protections.[75]

Another issue raised in opposition to S. 1925 was the lack of accountability for VAWA grantees.[76] Over the last few years, the DOJ Office of the Inspector General has audited several OVW grantees. The audit reports have cited improper allocation of funds, untimely financial and progress reports, weaknesses in budget management, and other compliance issues.[77] While S. 1925 would require the OVW to establish a biennial conferral process with grantees and key stakeholders, a concern was raised that the proposed legislation would not adequately ensure accountability of grant recipients.[78]

The reauthorization of VAWA (H.R. 4970) has been met with some opposition in the House. Several concerns were raised during the markup of H.R. 4970 in the House Judiciary Committee. Some Members voiced concern over new restrictions for immigration provisions under VAWA.[79] Another issue raised in opposition to H.R. 4970 is the absence of special consideration for those

---

(...continued)

[72] S.Rept. 112-153.

[73] U.S. Congress, Senate Committee on the Judiciary, *Executive Business Meeting*, 112th Cong., 2nd sess., February 2, 2012.

[74] S.Rept. 112-153

[75] Although tribes are not bound by protections found in the U.S. Constitution (*Talton v. Mayes*, 163 U.S. 376 (1896)), there are similar statutory protections for criminal defendants in tribal courts. See 25 U.S.C. §1302(6). For additional information, see CRS Report R42488, *Tribal Criminal Jurisdiction over Non-Indians in the Violence Against Women Act (VAWA) Reauthorization and the SAVE Native Women Act*, by Jane M. Smith and Richard M. Thompson II.

[76] S.Rept. 112-153

[77] U.S. Department of Justice, Office of the Inspector General, Audit of the Office on Violence Against Women Cooperative Agreement Administered by Girls Educational and Mentoring Services: New York, New York, GR-70-12-003, March 2012, http://www.justice.gov/oig/grants/2012/g7012003.pdf; Audit of the Office on Violence Against Women Grants to Jane Doe, Inc.: Boston, Massachusetts, GR-70-11-005, August 2011, http://www.justice.gov/oig/grants/2011/g7011005r.pdf; Audit of Office on Violence Against Women Grants Awarded to the Montana Coalition Against Domestic and Sexual Violence: Helena, Montana, GR-60-11-001, October 2010, http://www.justice.gov/oig/grants/2010/g6011001.pdf; Office on Violence Against Women Services, Training, Officers, and Prosecution Grants Awarded to the Commonwealth of Virginia Department of Criminal Justice Services, GR-30-10-003, July 2010, http://www.justice.gov/oig/grants/2010/g3010003.pdf; and Office on Violence Against Women Legal Assistance for Victims Grant Program Administered by the Community Legal Aid Society, Inc.: Wilmington, Delaware, GR-70-10-005, July 2010.

[78] S.Rept. 112-153.

[79] See CRS Report R42477, *Immigration Provisions of the Violence Against Women Act (VAWA)*, by William A. Kandel.

---

who may be discriminated against based on gender identity or sexual orientation. Finally, some Members sought increased jurisdictional powers for American Indian tribes, similar to provisions in S. 1925.[80]

Unlike the Senate bill, H.R. 4970 contains provisions that would increase accountability for VAWA grantees, an issue that has been cited by critics. The bill would require grantees to submit information regarding other Federal grants the applicant has applied for during the preceding year and provide a list of Federal grants the applicant received during the five-year period preceding the current application. The bill would also require the Attorney General to coordinate the administration of grants within the DOJ. The bill contains additional provisions to ensure accountability.

---

[80] U.S. Congress, House Committee on the Judiciary, *Full Committee Markup of: H.R. 4970, the Violence Against Women Reauthorization Act of 2012*, 112th Cong., May 8, 2012.

# Appendix. Federal Programs Authorized by VAWA

The fundamental goals of VAWA are to prevent violent crime, respond to the needs of crime victims, learn more about violence against women, and change public attitudes about domestic violence. This comprehensive strategy involves a collaborative effort by the criminal justice system, social service agencies, research organizations, public health organizations, and various private organizations. VAWA has supported these efforts primarily through federal grant programs that provide funding to state, tribal, and local governments, nonprofit organizations, and universities.

**Table A-1** provides descriptions of VAWA programs. **Table A-2** provides a five-year funding history for these programs.

## Table A-1. Descriptions of Current VAWA Authorized Programs under the Department of Justice (DOJ) and Department of Health and Human Services (HHS)

| Program and U.S. Code Citation (by Administrative Agency) | Purposes and Goals | Organizations Eligible to Apply |
|---|---|---|
| **Office on Violence Against Women (DOJ)** | | |
| STOP (Services, Training, Officers, and Prosecutors) Grant Program (42 U.S.C. §3796gg and 28 C.F.R. §90) | The purpose of this formula grant program is to enhance advocacy and improve the criminal justice system's response to violent crimes against women. | States and territories.[a] |
| Grants to Encourage Arrest Policies and Enforcement of Protection Orders (42 U.S.C. §3796hh) | The purpose of this grant program is to encourage state, local, and tribal courts and governments to treat domestic violence, dating violence, stalking, and sexual assault as serious crimes. | States; territories; tribal governments; units of local government; and state, tribal, territorial, and local courts (including juvenile courts). |
| Civil Legal Assistance for Victims Grant Program (42 U.S.C. §3796gg–6) | The purpose of this grant program is to strengthen civil and criminal legal assistance for victims of sexual assault, stalking, domestic violence, and dating violence through innovative and collaborative programs. | Private, nonprofit organizations; tribal governments and organizations; territorial organizations; and publicly funded organizations not acting in a governmental capacity (e.g., law schools). |
| Grants to Indian Tribal Governments Program (42 U.S.C. §3796gg–10) | The goals of this grant program are to develop and enhance effective plans for tribal governments to respond to violence committed against American Indian women and improve services for these women; strengthen the tribal criminal justice system; create community education and prevention campaigns; address the needs of children who witness domestic violence; provide supervised visitation and safe exchange programs; and provide transitional housing assistance and legal assistance. | Tribal governments; designees of tribal governments. |

| Program and U.S. Code Citation (by Administrative Agency) | Purposes and Goals | Organizations Eligible to Apply |
|---|---|---|
| Rural Domestic Violence, Dating Violence, Sexual Assault, Stalking, and Child Abuse Enforcement Assistance (42 U.S.C. §13971) | The purpose of these grants is to enhance the safety of victims of domestic violence, dating violence, sexual assault, and stalking by supporting projects uniquely designed to address and prevent these crimes in rural jurisdictions. | States; territories; tribal governments; units of local government; nonprofit, public or private organizations, including tribal organizations.[b] |
| Transitional Housing Assistance Grants for Victims of Domestic Violence (42 U.S.C. §13975)[c] | The purpose of this grant program is to use a holistic, victim-centered approach to provide transitional housing services for victims of domestic violence, dating violence, sexual assault, and stalking, and to move them into permanent housing. | States; territories; tribal governments; units of local government; domestic violence and sexual assault victim service providers; domestic violence and sexual assault coalitions; and other nonprofit, nongovernmental organizations, or community-based and culturally specific organizations.[d] |
| Sexual Assault Services Program (42 U.S.C. §14043g and 42 U.S.C. §3796gg) | The purpose of these formula grants is to provide intervention, advocacy, accompaniment, support services, and related assistance for adult, youth, and child victims of sexual assault, family and household members of victims, and those collaterally affected by the sexual assault. | States; territories; and private, nonprofit organizations that focus primarily on culturally-specific communities.[e] |
| Consolidated Youth Oriented Program[f] | This program consolidates four VAWA authorized programs: Engaging Men and Youth in Prevention, Grants to Assist Children and Youth Exposed to Violence, Supporting Teens Through Education Program (STEP), and Services to Advocate and Respond to Youth. A new grant description is not yet available from OVW. | OVW has not yet determined organizations eligible for this program. |
| Safe Havens: Supervised Visitation and Support Program (42 U.S.C. §10420)[g] | The purpose of this grant program is to provide an opportunity for communities to support the supervised visitation and safe exchange of children in situations involving domestic violence, dating violence, child abuse, sexual assault, or stalking. | States; territories; and tribal governments. |
| Grants to Reduce Domestic Violence, Dating Violence, Sexual Assault, and Stalking on Campus Program (42 U.S.C. §14045b) | The purpose of this grant is to encourage institutions of higher education to adopt comprehensive, coordinated responses to domestic violence, dating violence, sexual assault, and stalking. | Institutions of higher education. |
| Education, Training and Services to End Violence Against and Abuse of Women with Disabilities (42 U.S.C. §3796gg–7) | The purpose of this grant program is to build the capacity to address the growing problem of domestic violence, sexual assault, and dating violence against individuals with disabilities. | States; territories; tribal governments or organizations; units of local government; nonprofit, nongovernmental victim service organizations.[h] |

| Program and U.S. Code Citation (by Administrative Agency) | Purposes and Goals | Organizations Eligible to Apply |
|---|---|---|
| Court Training and Improvements (42 U.S.C. §14043 et seq.) | The purpose of this grant is to improve court responses to adult and youth domestic violence, dating violence, sexual assault, and stalking. | Federal, state, tribal, territorial, or local courts or court-based programs; and national, state, tribal, territorial, or local private, nonprofit organizations with demonstrated expertise in developing and providing judicial education about domestic violence, dating violence, sexual assault, or stalking. |
| Enhanced Training and Service to End Violence and Abuse of Women Later in Life (42 U.S.C. §14041a) | The purpose of this grant program is to provide or enhance training and services for victims of elder abuse, neglect, or exploitation, including victims of domestic violence, dating violence, sexual assault, or stalking. | States; territories; tribal governments or organizations; units of local government; nonprofit, nongovernmental victim service organizations.[i] |
| Tribal Domestic Violence and Sexual Assault Coalitions Grant (42 U.S.C. §3796gg–1) | The purpose of this grant program is to increase awareness of domestic violence and sexual assault against American Indian and Alaska Native women; enhance the response to violence against women at the tribal, federal, and state levels; and identify and provide technical assistance to coalition membership and tribal communities to enhance access to essential services. | Tribal coalitions; and individuals and organizations proposing to create tribal coalitions. |
| Grant for National Resource Center on Workplace Responses to Assist Victims of Domestic and Sexual Violence (42 U.S.C. §14043f) | The purpose of this grant program is to provide for the establishment and operation of a national resource center on workplace responses to assist victims of domestic and sexual violence.[j] | Nonprofit organizations; and tribal organizations. |
| Services to Advocate and Respond to Youth (42 U.S.C. §14043c) | The purpose of this grant program is to fund projects that create and implement programs and services to respond to the needs of youth who are victims of domestic violence, dating violence, sexual assault, or stalking. | Nonprofit, nongovernmental organizations; community-based organizations; tribes; and tribal organizations.[k] |
| Children and Youth Exposed to Violence (42 U.S.C. §14043d–2) | The purpose of this grant program is to mitigate the effects of domestic violence, dating violence, sexual assault, and stalking on children and youth exposed to violence and reduce the risk of future victimization or perpetration of these crimes. | States; territories; tribal governments; units of local government; nonprofit, victim service organizations; community-based organizations; and tribal organizations.[l] |
| Engaging Men and Youth in Preventing Domestic Violence, Dating Violence, Sexual Assault, and Stalking (42 U.S.C. §14043d–4) | The purpose of this grant program is to fund projects that develop or enhance efforts to engage men in preventing crimes of domestic violence, dating violence, sexual assault and stalking with the goal of developing mutually respectful, nonviolent relationships. | States; territories; tribal governments; units of local government; nonprofit, nongovernmental domestic violence, dating violence, sexual assault, or stalking victim service providers or coalitions; community-based child or youth service organizations.[m] |

| Program and U.S. Code Citation (by Administrative Agency) | Purposes and Goals | Organizations Eligible to Apply |
|---|---|---|
| Supporting Teens through Education and Protection (STEP) (42 U.S.C. §14043c–3) | The purpose of this grant program is to support projects that provide training to school personnel; develop policies and procedures for response; provide support services; develop effective prevention strategies; and collaborate with mentoring organizations to support middle and high school students who are victims of domestic violence, dating violence, sexual assault, or stalking. | State, local, tribal, and territorial courts; public, private, and military high schools and middle schools.[n] |
| **Office of Justice Programs (DOJ)** | | |
| Court Appointed Special Advocates for Victims of Child Abuse (42 U.S.C. §13013 et seq.)[o] | The purpose of this grant program is to provide trained individuals who are appointed by judges to advocate for the best interest of children who are involved in the juvenile and family court system due to abuse or neglect.[p] | National organizations.[q] |
| Training Programs to Assist Probation and Parole Officers (42 U.S.C. §13941) | The purpose of this program is to establish criteria and develop training programs to assist probation and parole officers and other personnel who work with released sex offenders in the areas of case management, supervision, and relapse prevention. | NA |
| Violence Against Women and Family Research and Evaluation Program (NIJ)[r] | The purpose of this research program is to promote the safety of women and family members, and to increase the efficiency and effectiveness of the criminal justice system's response to these crimes. | NA |
| Research on Violence Against Indian Women, National Baseline Study (NIJ) (42 U.S.C. §3796gg–10 Note) | The purpose of this program is to examine violence against American Indian and Alaska Native women and identify factors that place this population at risk for victimization; evaluate the effectiveness of federal, state, tribal, and local responses to violence against American Indian and Alaska Native women; and propose recommendations to improve effectiveness of these responses. | NA |
| National Stalker and Domestic Violence Reduction (42 U.S.C. §14031 et seq.) | The purpose of this program is to improve processes for entering data on stalking and domestic violence into local, state, and national crime information databases. | States; and units of local government.[s] |
| Tracking of Violence Against Women: National Tribal Sex Offender Registry (28 U.S.C. §534 Note) | The purpose of this program is to develop and maintain a national tribal sex offender registry. | Tribal governments; and tribal organizations. |

## Program and U.S. Code Citation (by Administrative Agency)

### Centers for Disease Control and Prevention (HHS)

| Program and U.S. Code Citation (by Administrative Agency) | Purposes and Goals | Organizations Eligible to Apply |
|---|---|---|
| Rape Prevention and Education Grant Program (42 U.S.C. §280b–1b) | The purpose of this program is to is to strengthen sexual violence prevention efforts in the states and territories. The goal is to increase awareness about sexual violence through educational seminars, hotline operations, and development of informational materials. | States and territories. |

**Sources:** Descriptions of grant programs' purposes and goals are taken from statute; the Office on Violence Against Women (OVW), available at http://www.ovw.usdoj.gov/ovwgrantprograms.htm#11; National Institute of Justice, available at http://www.nij.gov/topics/crime/violence-against-women/welcome.htm; National Resource Center on Workplace Responses, available at http://www.workplacesrespond.org; and the Centers for Disease Control and Prevention (CDC), available at http://www.cdc.gov/ViolencePrevention/RPE/. The organizations eligible to apply for grants are taken from the relevant statute and the *OVW Fiscal Year 2011 Grant Program Solicitation Reference Guide*, available at http://www.ovw.usdoj.gov/docs/resource-guidebook.pdf and from the RPE Grant Program description available at http://www.cdc.gov/ViolencePrevention/RPE/.

**Notes:** Programs in this table represent current programs that were authorized by the Violence Against Women and Department of Justice Reauthorization Act of 2005 (VAWA 2005, P.L. 109-162) and A Bill to Make Technical Corrections to the Violence Against Women and Department of Justice Reauthorization Act of 2005 (P.L. 109-271). Programs that did not receive appropriations in FY2010-FY2012 are not included in this table. Programs that are funded by set-asides from VAWA authorized programs are reflected in this table. See **Table A-2** for an outline of all programs authorized by VAWA 2005.

a.  Indian tribal governments, units of local government, and nonprofit, nongovernmental victim service programs may receive sub-grants from states.

b.  All applicants must propose to serve a rural area, as defined in statute.

c.  This program was originally authorized by the Prosecutorial Remedies and Other Tools to End the Exploitation of Children Today (PROTECT) Act of 2003 (P.L. 108-21), and was reauthorized by the Violence Against Women and Department of Justice Reauthorization Act of 2005.

d.  These organizations must have a documented history of effective work concerning domestic violence, dating violence, sexual assault, or stalking to carry out programs to provide assistance to minors, adults, and their dependents who are homeless, or in need of transitional housing or other housing assistance, as a result of fleeing a situation of domestic violence, dating violence, sexual assault, or stalking and for whom emergency shelter services or other crisis intervention services are unavailable or insufficient.

e.  These organizations must (1) have documented organizational experience in the area of sexual assault intervention or have entered into a partnership with an organization having such expertise; (2) have expertise in the development of community-based, linguistically and culturally specific outreach and intervention services relevant for the specific communities to whom assistance would be provided or have the capacity to link to existing services in the community tailored to the needs of culturally specific populations; and (3) have an advisory board or steering committee and staffing which is reflective of the targeted culturally specific community.

f.  The Consolidated Youth Oriented Program is not defined in statute. This program consolidates four VAWA-authorized programs in the Office on Violence Against Women: Engaging Men and Youth in Prevention, Grants to Assist Children and Youth Exposed to Violence, Supporting Teens Through Education Program (STEP), and Services to Advocate and Respond to Youth.

g.  This program was originally authorized by the Victims of Trafficking and Violence Protection Act of 2000 (P.L. 106-386). It was modified and reauthorized by the Violence Against Women Reauthorization Act of 2005.

h. Examples of organizations include state domestic violence or sexual assault coalitions and nonprofit, nongovernmental organizations that serve disabled individuals.

i. These organizations must have demonstrated experience in assisting elderly women or demonstrated experience in addressing domestic violence, dating violence, sexual assault, and stalking.

j. This grant currently funds The Workplaces Respond to Domestic and Sexual Violence: A National Resource Center Project. This project offers information to those interested in providing effective workplace responses to victims of domestic violence, sexual violence, dating violence and stalking.

k. Nonprofit, nongovernmental organizations must either (1) have the primary purpose of providing services to teen and young adult victims of domestic violence, dating violence, sexual assault, or stalking or (2) provide services for runaway or homeless youth affected by domestic or sexual abuse. Tribes and tribal organizations must provide services primarily to tribal youth or tribal victims of domestic violence, dating violence, sexual assault or stalking.

l. A state, local, or tribal government is only eligible if it is partnered with an eligible organization. Eligible organizations must have a documented history of effective work concerning children or youth exposed to domestic violence, dating violence, sexual assault, or stalking, including programs that provide culturally specific services, Head Start, childcare, faith-based organizations, after school programs, and health and mental health providers.

m. A state, local, or tribal government is only eligible if it is partnered with an eligible organization or a program that provides culturally specific services. Community-based organizations must have demonstrated experience and expertise in addressing the needs and concerns of young people. Organizations eligible to create public education campaigns and community organizing must have a documented history of creating and administering effective public education campaigns addressing the prevention of domestic violence, dating violence, sexual assault or stalking.

n. Schools are only eligible if they are partnered with (1) a domestic violence victim service provider that has a history of working on domestic violence and the impact that domestic violence and dating violence have on children and youth; and (2) a sexual assault victim service provider, such as a rape crisis center, program serving tribal victims of sexual assault, or coalition or other nonprofit, nongovernmental organization carrying out a community-based sexual assault program, that has a history of effective work concerning sexual assault and the impact that sexual assault has on children and youth. Schools may also partner with a law enforcement agency, courts, organizations and service providers addressing sexual harassment, bullying or gang-related violence in schools, and any other such agencies or organizations with the capacity to provide effective assistance to the adult, youth, and minor victims served by the partnership.

o. This program was originally authorized by the Victims of Child Abuse Act (P.L. 101-647). In 1994, 2000, and 2005, VAWA has reauthorized funding for this program.

p. The National Court Appointed Special Advocate (CASA) Program has received this award each year and makes sub-grants, on a competitive base, to local CASA programs. The CASA Program also provides training and technical assistance. For additional information, see http://www.casaforchildren.org.

q. National organizations must have broad membership among court-appointed special advocates, and must have demonstrated experience in grant administration of court-appointed special advocate programs and in providing training and technical assistance to court-appointed special advocate program. The organization may be may be a local public or nonprofit agency that has demonstrated the willingness to initiate, sustain, and expand a court-appointed special advocate program.

r. This program is not authorized by VAWA. It is included in this table because it is funded by a set-aside from the STOP Program.

s. States and local units of government must certify that it has or intends to establish a program that enters into the National Crime Information Center records of warrants, arrests, convictions and protection orders.

## Table A-2. FY2008-FY2012 Authorization and Appropriations for VAWA Programs

(dollars in millions)

| Grant Programs and U.S. Code Citation (by Administrative Agency) | FY2008 | | FY2009 | | FY2010 | | FY2011 | | FY2012 | |
|---|---|---|---|---|---|---|---|---|---|---|
| | Authorized | Enacted | Authorized | Enacted | Authorized | Enacted | Authorized | Enacted | Authorized | Enacted |
| **Office on Violence Against Women (DOJ)** | | | | | | | | | | |
| STOP (Services, Training, Officers, and Prosecutors) Grant Program (42 U.S.C. §3793(a)(18)) | $225.00 | $183.80 | $225.00 | $365.00[ab] | $225.00 | $210.00[c] | $225.00 | $209.58[d] | — | $189.00 |
| Grants to Encourage Arrest Policies and Enforcement of Protection Orders (42 U.S.C. §3793(a)(19)) | 75.00 | 59.22 | 75.00 | 60.00 | 75.00 | 60.00 | 75.00 | 59.88 | — | 50.00 |
| Civil Legal Assistance for Victims Grant Program (42 U.S.C. §3796gg–6) | 65.00 | 36.66 | 65.00 | 37.00 | 65.00 | 41.00 | 65.00 | 40.92 | — | 41.00 |
| Tribal Governments Program (42 U.S.C. §3796gg–10 and 42 U.S.C. §3796gg–1) | [e] | — | [e] | — | [e] | (38.97) | [e] | (37.40) | [e] | (35.27) |

| Grant Programs and U.S. Code Citation (by Administrative Agency) | FY2008 | | FY2009 | | FY2010 | | FY2011 | | FY2012 | |
|---|---|---|---|---|---|---|---|---|---|---|
| | Authorized | Enacted | Authorized | Enacted | Authorized | Enacted | Authorized | Enacted | Authorized | Enacted |
| Rural Domestic Violence, Dating Violence, Sexual Assault, Stalking, and Child Abuse Enforcement Assistance (42 U.S.C. §13971) | 55.00 | 40.42 | 55.00 | 41.00 | 55.00 | 41.00 | 55.00 | 40.92 | — | 34.00 |
| Transitional Housing Assistance Grants for Victims of Domestic Violence (42 U.S.C. §13975)[f] | 40.00 | (17.39)[g] | 40.00 | (68.00)[gh] | 40.00 | (18.00)[g] | 40.00 | (17.96)[g] | — | 25.00 |
| Sexual Assault Services Program (42 U.S.C. §14043g) | 50.00 | 9.40 | 50.00 | 12.00 | 50.00 | 15.00 | 50.00 | 14.97 | — | 23.00 |
| Consolidated Youth Oriented Program[i] | i | — | i | — | i | — | i | — | i | 10.00 |
| Safe Havens: Supervised Visitation and Support Program (42 U.S.C. §10420)[j] | 20.00 | 13.63 | 20.00 | 14.00 | 20.00 | 14.00 | 20.00 | 13.97 | — | 11.50 |

| Grant Programs and U.S. Code Citation (by Administrative Agency) | FY2008 | | FY2009 | | FY2010 | | FY2011 | | FY2012 | |
|---|---|---|---|---|---|---|---|---|---|---|
| | Authorized | Enacted | Authorized | Enacted | Authorized | Enacted | Authorized | Enacted | Authorized | Enacted |
| Grants to Reduce Domestic Violence, Dating Violence, Sexual Assault, and Stalking on Campus Program (42 U.S.C. §14045b) | 15.00 | 9.40 | 15.00 | 9.50 | 15.00 | 9.50 | 15.00 | 9.48 | — | 9.00 |
| Education, Training and Services to End Violence Against and Abuse of Women with Disabilities (42 U.S.C. §3796gg–7) | 10.00 | 6.58 | 10.00 | 6.75 | 10.00 | 6.75 | 10.00 | 6.74 | — | 5.75 |
| Court Training and Improvements Program (42 U.S.C. §14043a-3) | 5.00 | 2.80 | 5.00 | 3.00 | 5.00 | 3.00 | 5.00 | 2.99 | — | 4.50 |
| Enhanced Training and Service to End Violence and Abuse of Women Later in Life Program (42 U.S.C. §14041b) | 10.00 | 4.23 | 10.00 | 4.25 | 10.00 | 4.25 | 10.00 | 4.24 | — | 4.25 |

| Grant Programs and U.S. Code Citation (by Administrative Agency) | FY2008 | | FY2009 | | FY2010 | | FY2011 | | FY2012 | |
|---|---|---|---|---|---|---|---|---|---|---|
| | Authorized | Enacted | Authorized | Enacted | Authorized | Enacted | Authorized | Enacted | Authorized | Enacted |
| Tribal Domestic Violence and Sexual Assault Coalitions Grant Program (42 U.S.C. §3796gg—1) | k | — | k | (3.93)[l] | k | (3.93)[l] | k | (3.92)[l] | — | (3.93)[l] |
| Grant for National Resource Center on Workplace Responses to Assist Victims of Domestic and Sexual Violence (42 U.S.C. §14043f) | 1.00 | 0.90 | 1.00 | 1.00 | 1.00 | 1.00 | 1.00 | 1.00 | | 1.00 |
| Indian Country Sexual Assault Clearinghouse[m] | — | — | — | — | — | — | — | — | [n] | 0.50 |
| Services to Advocate and Respond to Youth (42 U.S.C. §14043c) | 15.00 | 2.82 | 15.00 | 3.50 | 15.00 | 3.50 | 15.00 | 3.49 | — | [o] |
| Children and Youth Exposed to Violence (42 U.S.C. §14043d-2) | 20.00 | 2.82 | 20.00 | 3.00 | 20.00 | 3.00 | 20.00 | 3.00 | — | [o] |

| Grant Programs and U.S. Code Citation (by Administrative Agency) | FY2008 | | FY2009 | | FY2010 | | FY2011 | | FY2012 | |
|---|---|---|---|---|---|---|---|---|---|---|
| | Authorized | Enacted | Authorized | Enacted | Authorized | Enacted | Authorized | Enacted | Authorized | Enacted |
| Engaging Men and Youth in Preventing Domestic Violence, Dating Violence, Sexual Assault, and Stalking (42 U.S.C. §14043d-4) | 10.00 | 2.82 | 10.00 | 3.00 | 10.00 | 3.00 | 10.00 | 2.99 | — | ° |
| Supporting Teens through Education and Protection (STEP) (42 U.S.C. §14043c-3) | 5.00 | — | 5.00 | — | 5.00 | 2.50 | 5.00 | 2.50 | — | ° |
| Grants to Combat Violence Against Women in Public and Assisted Housing (42 U.S.C. §14043e-4) | 10.00 | — | 10.00 | — | 10.00 | — | 10.00 | — | — | — |
| Development of Curricula and Pilot Programs for Home Visitation Projects (42 U.S.C. §14043d-3) | 7.00 | — | 7.00 | — | 7.00 | — | 7.00 | — | — | — |
| Access to Justice for Youth (42 U.S.C. §14043c-1) | 5.00 | — | 5.00 | — | 5.00 | — | 5.00 | — | — | — |

| Grant Programs and U.S. Code Citation (by Administrative Agency) | FY2008 | | FY2009 | | FY2010 | | FY2011 | | FY2012 | |
|---|---|---|---|---|---|---|---|---|---|---|
| | Authorized | Enacted | Authorized | Enacted | Authorized | Enacted | Authorized | Enacted | Authorized | Enacted |
| Grants to Protect the Privacy and Confidentiality of Victims of Domestic and Dating Violence, Sexual Assault, and Stalking (42 U.S.C. §14043b-4) | 5.00 | — | 5.00 | — | 5.00 | — | 5.00 | — | — | — |
| Grants for Outreach to Underserved Populations (42 U.S.C. §14045) | 2.00 | — | 2.00 | — | 2.00 | — | 2.00 | — | — | — |
| Public Awareness Campaign (42 U.S.C. §14045c) | p | — | p | — | p | — | — | — | — | — |
| **Office of Justice Programs (DOJ)** | | | | | | | | | | |
| Court Appointed Special Advocates for Victims of Child Abuse (42 U.S.C. §13014) | 12.00 | 13.16 | 12.00 | 15.00 | 12.00 | 15.00 | 12.00 | 12.43 | — | 4.50 |
| Violence Against Women and Family Research and Evaluation Program (NIJ)q | q | (1.90) | q | (1.88) | q | (3.00) | q | (3.00) | — | 3.00 |

| Grant Programs and U.S. Code Citation (by Administrative Agency) | FY2008 | | FY2009 | | FY2010 | | FY2011 | | FY2012 | |
|---|---|---|---|---|---|---|---|---|---|---|
| | Authorized | Enacted | Authorized | Enacted | Authorized | Enacted | Authorized | Enacted | Authorized | Enacted |
| Research on Violence Against Indian Women, National Baseline Study (NIJ) (42 U.S.C. §3796gg–10 Note) | 1.00 | 0.90 | — | 1.00 | — | 1.00 | — | 0.80 | — | 1.00 |
| Training Programs to Assist Probation and Parole Officers (42 U.S.C. §13941) | 5.00 | 3.29 | 5.00 | 3.50 | 5.00 | 3.50 | 5.00 | 2.90 | — | — |
| National Stalker and Domestic Violence Reduction (42 U.S.C. §14032) | 3.00 | 2.80 | 3.00 | 3.00 | 3.00 | 3.00 | 3.00 | 2.49 | — | — |
| Tracking of Violence Against Women: National Tribal Sex Offender Registry (28 U.S.C. §534 Note) | 1.00 | 0.90 | 1.00 | 1.00 | 1.00 | 1.00 | 1.00 | 1.00 | — | — |
| **Executive Office of U.S. Attorneys (DOJ)** | | | | | | | | | | |
| Federal Victim Assistants[r] | 1.00 | — | 1.00 | — | 1.00 | — | 1.00 | — | — | — |
| **Undetermined Agency (DOJ)**[s] | | | | | | | | | | |

| Grant Programs and U.S. Code Citation (by Administrative Agency) | FY2008 | | FY2009 | | FY2010 | | FY2011 | | FY2012 | |
|---|---|---|---|---|---|---|---|---|---|---|
| | Authorized | Enacted | Authorized | Enacted | Authorized | Enacted | Authorized | Enacted | Authorized | Enacted |
| Grants for Law Enforcement Training (42 U.S.C. 14044f) | 10.00 | — | 10.00 | — | 10.00 | — | 10.00 | — | — | — |
| *Subtotal for DOJ:* | 683.00 | 396.55 | 682.00 | 586.50 | 682.00 | 441.00 | 682.00 | 436.29 | — | 417.00 |
| **Centers for Disease Control and Prevention (HHS)** | | | | | | | | | | |
| Rape Prevention and Education Grants (42 U.S.C. §280b–1b) | 80.00 | 42.02 | 80.00 | 41.84 | 80.00 | 42.62 | 80.00 | 39.47 | — | 37.90 |
| Grants to Foster Public Health Responses to Domestic Violence, Dating Violence, Sexual Assault, and Stalking (42 U.S.C. §280g–4)[t] | 5.00 | — | 5.00 | — | 5.00 | — | 5.00 | — | — | — |
| Research on Effective Interventions in the Healthcare Setting (42 U.S.C. §13973)[t] | 5.00 | — | 5.00 | — | 5.00 | — | 5.00 | — | — | — |

| Grant Programs and U.S. Code Citation (by Administrative Agency) | FY2008 | | FY2009 | | FY2010 | | FY2011 | | FY2012 | |
|---|---|---|---|---|---|---|---|---|---|---|
| | Authorized | Enacted | Authorized | Enacted | Authorized | Enacted | Authorized | Enacted | Authorized | Enacted |
| Study Conducted by the Centers for Disease Control and Prevention (42 U.S.C. §280b–4) | 2.00 | — | 2.00 | — | 2.00 | — | — | — | — | — |
| **Centers for Disease Control and Prevention and Indian Health Service (HHS)** | | | | | | | | | | |
| Analysis and Research on Violence Against Indian Women, Injury Study[u] | 0.50 | — | 0.50 | — | — | — | — | — | — | — |
| **Administration for Children and Families (HHS)** | | | | | | | | | | |
| Collaborative Grants to Increase the Long-Term Stability of Victims (42 U.S.C. §14043e–3) | 10.00 | — | 10.00 | — | 10.00 | — | 10.00 | — | — | — |

| Grant Programs and U.S. Code Citation (by Administrative Agency) | FY2008 Authorized | FY2008 Enacted | FY2009 Authorized | FY2009 Enacted | FY2010 Authorized | FY2010 Enacted | FY2011 Authorized | FY2011 Enacted | FY2012 Authorized | FY2012 Enacted |
|---|---|---|---|---|---|---|---|---|---|---|
| Grants for Training and Collaboration on the Intersection Between Domestic Violence and Child Maltreatment (Family and Youth Services Bureau) (42 U.S.C. §14043c–2) | 5.00 | — | 5.00 | — | 5.00 | — | 5.00 | — | — | — |
| **Health Resources and Services Administration (HHS)** | | | | | | | | | | |
| Interdisciplinary Training and Education on Domestic Violence and Other Types of Violence and Abuse (42 U.S.C. §294h)^c | 3.00 | — | 3.00 | — | 3.00 | — | 3.00 | — | — | — |
| *Subtotal for HHS* | 110.50 | 42.02 | 110.50 | 41.84 | 110.00 | 42.62 | 108.00 | 39.47 | — | 37.90 |
| *Subtotal for DOJ* | 683.00 | 396.55 | 682.00 | 586.50 | 682.00 | 441.00 | 682.00 | 436.29 | — | 417.00 |
| **Total** | **793.50** | **438.57** | **792.50** | **628.34** | **792.00** | **483.62** | **790.00** | **475.76** | **—** | **454.90** |

**Sources:** FY2008-FY2012 appropriations for the OVW and OJP were taken from the congressional budget submissions for the OVW and OJP. The FY2008 and FY2009 appropriations for the CDC were taken from S.Rept. 110-410. The FY2010-FY2012 appropriations for the CDC were provided by the CDC.

**Notes:** This table includes programs authorized in the most recent reauthorization of VAWA (P.L. 109-162) and subsequent amendment to VAWA (P.L. 109-271). This table includes VAWA authorized programs that did not receive appropriations. Programs that are funded by set-asides from VAWA authorized programs are reflected in this table and marked with parentheses.

a.  This amount includes $225.00 million provided by the American Recovery and Reinvestment Act of 2009 (P.L. 111-5).

b.  For FY2009, enacted funding for the STOP Program includes set-asides of $1.88 million for the Violence Against Women and Family Research and Evaluation Program (NIJ) and $18.00 million for the Transitional Housing Assistance Program.

c.  For FY2010, the enacted funding for the STOP Program includes set-asides of $3.00 million for the Violence Against Women and Family Research and Evaluation Program (NIJ) and $18.00 million for the Transitional Housing Assistance Program.

d.  For FY2011, the enacted funding for the STOP Program includes set-asides of $2.99 million for the Violence Against Women and Family Research and Evaluation Program (NIJ) and $17.96 million for the Transitional Housing Assistance Program.

e.  The Tribal Governments Program is funded by set-asides from seven other OVW grant programs: STOP; Grants to Encourage Arrest Policies and Enforcement of Protection Orders; Rural Domestic Violence, Dating Violence, Sexual Assault, Stalking, and Child Abuse Enforcement Assistance; Civil Legal Assistance for Victims; Safe Havens; Transitional Housing; and Court Training and Improvements.

f.  This program was originally authorized by the Prosecutorial Remedies and Other Tools to End the Exploitation of Children Today (PROTECT) Act of 2003 (P.L. 108-21), and was reauthorized by the Violence Against Women and Department of Justice Reauthorization Act of 2005.

g.  For FY2008-FY2011, this program was funded by set-asides from the STOP Program.

h.  This amount includes emergency supplemental appropriations of $50.00 million provided under The American Recovery and Reinvestment Act of 2009 (P.L. 111-5).

i.  This program is not authorized by VAWA. It consolidates four VAWA-authorized programs in the Office on Violence Against Women: Engaging Men and Youth in Prevention, Grants to Assist Children and Youth Exposed to Violence, Supporting Teens Through Education Program (STEP), and Services to Advocate and Respond to Youth.

j.  This grant was originally authorized by the Victims of Trafficking and Violence Protection Act of 2000 (P.L. 106-386). It was modified and reauthorized by the Violence Against Women and Department of Justice Reauthorization Act of 2005.

k.  Congress did not specify an amount of funding for this program but authorized set-asides from the STOP Program and Sexual Assault Services Program.

l.  The Tribal Domestic Violence and Sexual Assault Coalitions Program is funded by statutory set-asides from the STOP Program and Sexual Assault Services Program.

m.  This program does not have a U.S. Code citation.

n.  This program is not authorized by VAWA. Congress established this program under the Consolidated and Further Continuing Appropriations Act, 2012 (P.L. 112-55) for the purpose of providing training and technical assistance on issues relating to sexual assault of American Indian and Alaska Native women.

o.  This program is one of four programs consolidated to create the Consolidated Youth Oriented Program. FY2012 funding for this program is reflected in the FY2012 funding for the Consolidated Youth Oriented Program.

p.  The Violence Against Women and Department of Justice Reauthorization Act of 2005 authorized "sums as may be necessary" for FY2006-FY2010.

q.  This program is not authorized by VAWA. It is included in this table because it was funded by a set-aside from the STOP Program from FY2008-FY2011. In FY2012, it received a direct appropriation.

r.  This program does not have a U.S. Code citation but funding is authorized under Sec. 110 of the Violence Against Women and Department of Justice Reauthorization Act of 2005.

s.  The Attorney General has not yet determined the administrative office for the Grants for Law Enforcement Training Program.

t.  These programs were never funded, however, the basic purpose areas were funded through an appropriations provision with grants administered by the HHS Office of Women's Health (OWH). For additional information, see http://www.womenshealth.gov/violence-against-women/.

u.  This program does not have a U.S. Code citation but funding is authorized under Sec. 904 of the Violence Against Women and Department of Justice Reauthorization Act of 2000

# Author Contact Information

Lisa M. Seghetti
Section Research Manager
lseghetti@crs.loc.gov, 7-4669

Jerome P. Bjelopera
Specialist in Organized Crime and Terrorism
jbjelopera@crs.loc.gov, 7-0622

# Acknowledgment

Lisa N. Sacco, Analyst in Illicit Drugs and Crime Policy, was the original author of this report.

www.ingramcontent.com/pod-product-compliance
Lightning Source LLC
Chambersburg PA
CBHW082201290526
45794CB00008B/3382